This book belongs to

_____

This book is written just in a humorous way about a fun adventure a little girl goes on in her dream.

News flash! There is someone stealing some chocolate from
Candy Land.
Can Katherine help find out who it is?
A candy bar and chocolate eggs goes missing each day.
The only clues are some strange footprints...
These are the footprints.
Who could it be?

Candy Land was in trouble! Katherine noticed that there were chocolate eggs and bonbons thrown into the river! Who could be playing such a trick?
Where does the river lead? Maybe that can help, if we know where the chocolate will end up.

Let's follow the river.

Well, this is interesting! I see so many rabbits. I must be in Rabbit Valley now.
"Have any of you noticed anyone strange in the area that could be stealing our chocolates?" Katherine asked.
All the rabbits thought for a moment, and they all said,
"NOPE. Sorry, nothing strange or unusual here."
Maybe, I can ask at Chocolate Towers, she thought.

"Hello Chocolate Towers.
Have you seen anything strange
or unusual this week?"

"NOPE – Sorry. Nothing here."
Maybe, I can check Runaway
Lane she thought.

Runaway Lane was a cool place. This is where we could run and jump into the melted chocolate river.
It was always warm. Katherine thinks she can see something in the distance.
What,
or who,
could it be?

My sister Charlotte!
It is you!
You have been eating all the chocolate.....

And then I woke up from my dream. Now I am hungry for CHOCOLATE!
~ The end

What happens next?

Use the next pages section to write your own fun dream, or a continued part of this dream. There are characters you can add into the story as you go.

The end

www.ingramcontent.com/pod-product-compliance
Lightning Source LLC
Chambersburg PA
CBHW041758040426
42446CB00005B/243